GOATS

Meat, fibre, dairy and more

GOATS

Meat, fibre, dairy and more

Margaret Muir

ISBN – 978-1514824177
ISBN-10: 1514824175

Acknowledgement

I wish to thank Tambookie Boer Goat Stud for allowing me to use pictures of their Boer Goats in this book.
For more information about Tambookie Boer Goat Stud visit:
https://tambookieboergoatstud.wordpress.com *or follow them on Facebook.*

Author's note

While the inclusion of images in this publication has been limited, the electronic (Amazon Kindle) edition of this book has considerably more illustrations.

Much of the original content of this book, written by the author, was published in the New Zealand Goat Farmer Magazine. At the time of writing, the author ran a herd of angora goats. She has also bred Boer Goats for stud, meat and the live-goat export markets from Australia.

Table of Contents

South African Boer Buck

(Photo – MM)

Introduction

Over 10,000 thousand years ago, the humble goat, which originated in the arid regions of Turkey and Iran, was one of the first animals to be domesticated. With its ability to thrive in harsh environments and its tolerance of humans, it was valued as a source of milk, meat, fibre and leather.

As western civilizations extend their boundaries, goats were transported around the globe and, over the years, were released or escaped into new areas. Unfortunately, because of their ability to adapt, goats survived, thrived and multiplied. In some areas, overgrazing by large herds caused severe environmental damage and goats were regarded as feral pests to be captured, shot or poisoned.

In the last 30 years, however, as the true value of these animals has again been acknowledged, a change in attitude has slowly come about. If properly managed, goats not only continue to provide meat, fibre, milk and leather but also a good income for the serious farmer who is prepared to work with them and not against them.

Chapter 1

The Boer Goat – its history, its features and qualities

Background

(Tambookie Boer Goats - does)

The South African Improved or Ennobled Boer goat is the only true meat goat in the world. It represents the culmination of 50 years specialized breeding in its homeland for improved meat quality and quantity.

The breed was not created from two or more pure breeds, as is the case with other varieties of animals bred in South Africa. Rather, the prototype for the breed was selected from all existing breeds of goats in South Africa in order to achieve the functional characteristics and type as they are today – hence the name Improved or Ennobled Boer goat. (The Improved Boer Goat Brochure – no date or author)

The Boer Goat Association of South Africa was founded in 1959 and the breed standard was set at that time, but it was not until the 1990 that the association allowed any of its Boers to leave the country. Prior to that all its goat meat was consumed by the home market and neither goats nor meat were exported from South Africa.

The first Boer goats to arrive in the US in the 1990s came into the country from Canada or directly from South Africa, or were imported via New Zealand.

The Improved breed was first released into Australia in April 1995 after the imported animals had undergone the mandatory seven years quarantine period to ensure they were not carrying the disease Scrapie (related to the devastating encephalopathy–Mad Cow Disease). Introduction of this wasting disease would spell disaster to the Australian sheep industry which the country relies on so heavily.

After completing the stipulated time, the original imports were destroyed and their brains examined for any traces of the disease. Only the progeny of those goats that were born on the quarantine station were released to the stud breeders who had been patiently awaiting them.

In Australia, *goat* was once a dirty word. The cockies (farmers) hated them. However, the introduction of the Boer goat led to a complete turn-around in attitude. Within a decade of their arrival, farmers and graziers were looking at the vast number of feral goats in a different light. From an animal that was long despised, poisoned and shot by the thousands in large-scale and expensive eradication programs, cross-bred meat goats, sired by Boers, were soon to become a profitable and accepted commercial enterprise in the pastoral station country.

Properties of the Boer Goat

With a docile nature, Boer goats are intelligent and easy to manage gentle-giants. The mature bucks can grow to 135 kg in weight and does to 95 kg.

Males (bucks/rams/billys) demonstrate high fecundity (able to serve 40 does easily), while females (does/ewes/nannies) are capable of kidding three times a year and usually produce twins or often triplets. The does also have excellent mothering qualities.

The weight gain recorded in Boer kids is the fastest of all small ruminants. Early Australian trials using Boer bucks over feral does showed an increase of 40% in carcase weight of first-cross Boer kids as against feral kids.

Desirable physical features of a Boer goat

- A strong red head and neck with a broad white blaze running down the curved forehead and nose.
- A pair of strong rounded horns bent backwards. An all-white body with a well fleshed broad barrel.
- Darkly pigmented skin (visible around the anus).
- The coat should be short and slightly glossy. The skin should be supple and folded around the neck (on the bucks).
- Sturdy legs with strong feet and hoofs.

Farming Boer goats

Goats are browsers not grazers. Sheep eat pasture from ground level to 5 inches above, whereas goats prefer to browse on anything 5 inches above the ground. Experiments have proved that Boers eat 74% leaves, woody bushes and shrubs and only 26% grasses. Therefore, goats are ideal to run with cattle without being in direct competition.

Because goats eat thorny plants, such as blackberry plus other hardy invasive vegetation, they are useful in clearing/controlling aggressive weeds.

With good feet and strong hoofs, they are hardy and adaptable and can cover long distances over hard ground or rocky surfaces.

They are relatively disease resistant.

Boer goats are not labour intensive and production costs are low with no shearing, crutching or mulesing necessary. (Mulesing is the removal of wool-bearing skin from round the anus and tail of a sheep to reduce the incidence of flystrike.)

Boer meat goats produce high quality meat with low fat content. They also produce quality skins with a high leather value.

(Small flock of Boer goats MM)

Chapter 2

GOAT MEAT (part 1) – CAPRETTO/CABRITO – What is the difference?

Goat meat has been eaten for millennia and is often referred to as Chevon derived from the French word *chèvre* (goat). This usually refers to the flesh of a mature animal. In some countries it is also called mutton.

The most tender meat, however, is from a milk-fed goat kid. It is eaten in many part of the world, is often regarded as a delicacy and is known by different names according to where you live.

CAPRETTO is the Italian name for kid goat. CABRITO if the Latin/Spanish name for the same.

By specification, Cabrito/Capretto is young milk-fed kid goat ranging from 12 to 20 weeks of age with a carcase dressed weight between 6 and 12 kg. The meat is very tender with a mild flavour similar to veal. It should be pale pink in colour. For the grower, it will return a premium price on the export market.

Cabrito is eaten as a specialty dish common in Latin cuisines such as in Mexico, Peru, Brazil and Argentina where it is usually slow roasted.

Capretto is most popular in southern Italy and Greece. It is an Easter celebration staple in the Alpine regions of central Europe. In the Bavarian Alps of Germany, it is served braised. In the Austrian Alps region it is usually crumbed and fried.

For centuries, young milk-fed kids slaughtered for meat were usually the unwanted male kids of dairy herds. However, by today's standards, dairy goats, especially Nubian-types, are the least desirable as they are often rather leggy.

Thirty years ago, in Australia, a booming export trade in kid carcases was established on the back of the cashmere industry. However, fibre production declined in 1990s following the release of the South African Boer Goat genetics into Australia.

Flocks of both feral and cashmere does were suddenly in demand for use as recipients for the new genetics through live mating, Artificial Insemination and embryo transplant programs.

Though initially, because of the value of the newly imported genetics, pure male Boer goat kids were kept and raised to be sold to stud breeders or exported as terminal sires, the cross-bred kids from the feral or cashmere does heralded the start of a burgeoning goat meat export industry. The improved conformation and meat qualities of the imported genetics were immediately evident in the cross-bred kids.

The Ennobled Boer goat had long been bred in South Africa as a meat animal.

(Boer doe with twins: MM)

The Boer's genetics relevant to Capretto/Cabrito carcases are as follows:

- Excellent conformation.
- High fecundity and increased kid production.

- Does average 160% weaned kids with kidding rates as high as 200%.
- Good mothering instincts in the does and high milk production for rearing kids resulting in high or early weaning.
- Kids show excellent growth rates and are therefore ready for market early. Kids average a daily weight gain of 255 grams per day.

Things to remember

In producing kids for the export market – the kids should remain on the doe until the time of slaughter in order to maintain the pale flesh meat colour.

Kids should be grown to meet the desired weight specifications. At the abattoir, overweight kids are heavily penalized (in price) if delivered for the export trade.

Once the kid is weaned and its diet changes, then the meat will darken and can no longer be marketed as Capretto/Cabrito. As it matures, the young goat is classed as Chevon.

Chapter 3

GOAT MEAT – CAPRETTO (cont'd) – meeting the European market

For more than a decade, Western Australian goat farmers supplied Capretto (Cabrito) to a niche export market in Europe. Growers knew exactly what the customer required and supplied to meet those demands. In return they are well paid for goat kids.

Prior to this, farmers got rid of the kids the best way they could. Goat breeders were selling kids for $2 to $3 each. However the local market could not consume all the meat that was available through the abattoirs.

While Cashmere producers were bringing in up to 1000 kids for slaughter, the financial returns were pathetic until two of the major farming bodies got together with the Meat Commission to find an overseas outlet for their produce. The market they found was Switzerland.

Despite buying 100,000 Capretto from France each year, the Swiss buyer placed a premium on the environmentally clean Australian grown commodity. Because most French Capretto comes from dairy goats, where quality control is often absent, the product lacked consistency, whereas West Australian farmers were able to produce true Capretto.

To satisfy the export specifications, farmers were required to supply kids in the live weight range 12–20 kilos. These dress out between 6–10 kilos, however, carcases in the 5–9 kilos are most desirable. The meat colour of the Capretto must be light (indicating the kid is milk-reared).

With the infusions of Boer genetics, kids can grow to the correct weight as early as 6 weeks of age and have a dressed weight of 54% of the live weight. This is a phenomenal percentage for any meat animal.

The kids delivered to the abattoir include feral/Boer crosses, angoras and cashmere-crosses plus dairy kids. The average age of receivals is ten weeks, however, dairy goat breeders experience problems with dairy kids that grow too big too quickly. Their body conformation is not as good as that of a Boer-type. Dairy kids result in a leggy carcase that is not attractive.

Farmers, supplying the export trade, were given a forward contract guaranteed price of $30 (Au) for Capretto, but were heavily penalized for kids outside the weight range. Overweight carcases of this type were rejected for export and sold on the local market. By penalizing in this manner, growers soon learned to meet the market standard. Under or oversized-carcases returned only $8.00. "We educate the growers by hitting them in the back pocket where it hurts the most," the coordinator said.

The export Capretto market runs from August to December (Southern Hemisphere Spring). Kid goats produced outside these months are sold on the domestic market.

In season, kids are received every Monday morning at the abattoir where up to 700 kids are processed in the day. The goats are killed soon after delivery and snap chilled and bagged. Two days later the carcases are sent to the processing plant where they are sorted. Small Capretto carcases are kept whole. Those over 7 kilos are chopped into cuts. These are then boxed and labelled.

Every week 70 carcases are flown directly to Europe. The remainder is stored frozen for transport by sea container. The first consignment is shipped from Australia to supply the Christmas market in Europe. The second delivery meets the Easter demand. In the season, approximately 10,000 Capretto are dispatched to Switzerland.

Kid production increased enormously after the introduction of the South African Boer genetics. At first only 2-3000 Capretto per year were being exported, but as the market became known, a few farmers started producing specifically to fill this market. The first large commercial breeder turned over 2000 kids each season.

This raised the possibility of supplying Capretto to other European or overseas markets where the demand is on-going.

Today the major Australian exporter of goat meat is Western Meat Exporters Pty Ltd situated at Charleville in South West Queensland, Australia (more in the chapter on Chevon/mutton).

Note: Weights and prices may have changed since this article was first published.

Chapter 4

GOAT MEAT (Part 2) – Chevon/mutton

The humble goat was probably the first animal to be domesticated, which is not surprising as it has so much to offer. Besides producing milk, goats provide fleece for spinning, skins for leather and nutritious red meat for human consumption.

Goat meat has been part of the diet of people around the world for thousands of years and, as such, goat meat is one of the few meats that is not discriminated against by religious taboos.

Goats are easy to raise and prolific breeders that can thrive on cultivated farms or in inhospitable environments. The meat they produce is slightly sweeter but similar in taste to lamb. It is also lean and healthy due to its low fat and cholesterol content (lower than sheep meat or chicken), and is lower in calories than port, beef or lamb.

Goat meat is higher than beef in iron and protein levels and, because of its molecular structure, goat meat is easier to digest. It is an ideal choice for health conscious meat lovers. For these reasons, goat meat is the most eaten red-meat in the world, however, the western world has been slow to develop a liking for the flavour.

The places most associated with goat cuisine are Africa, the Middle East, India, Nepal, Pakistan, Mexico, Taiwan and the Caribbean. On the Indian subcontinent *mutton* is the word used to describe both goat and sheep meat.

While kid goats are marketed as Capretto or Cabrito, two-tooth goats up to 16 months in age are larger than Capretto and are marketed as Chevon (from the French word *chèvre* meaning goat). The meat is slightly redder than kid goat but is still tender, juicy and has a good flavour. Goats over 16 months are classed as *goat* or *mutton*.

Adult goat's meat has a firm texture and the flavour is described as mild to strong depending on the sex and age of the animal. Weight can be used to assess the age of the goat although the various breeds vary considerably in size and weight.

Ceremonial slaughter

While goat meat is one of the few meats free from most religious taboos, it is demanded on special occasions for ceremonial purposes.

In Africa, the Chaga people of Tanzania kill, roast and eat a goat in a ceremonial tradition which has been practiced for hundreds of years. In some countries, a ceremonial goat is offered to guests at wedding ceremonies (in place of the western world's wedding cake).

For Muslims, the end of the sacred month of Ramadan is celebrated with the slaughter of a goat. Every man will kill a goat and provide meat for his family. By tradition, he will also give some meat to his relatives and to the poor.

Goat meat is also a major delicacy in Nepal where male goats are sacrificed during Dashain – a Hindu ceremony. At this event, the largest annual celebration in the country, buffalo and goats are sacrificed to appease the gods. These animal sacrifices commemorate the mythical bloody battles between divine and demonic powers. Again the sacrificial meat feeds the family.

Meet the world's largest goat meat exporter

Western Meat Exporters is considered the largest goat meat processor and exporter in the world. The company has been operating since August 1997 and is situated at Charleville in south-west Queensland, Australia.

One hundred percent of its meat products are exported and distributed worldwide to over 30 countries including the USA, European Union, Canada, Asia and the Middle East and India. The United States and Taiwan are the biggest customers. Australian goat meat arrives into the USA frozen and usually as whole carcases.

This specialist goat-only facility produces *Halal* meat to satisfy all its export markets and to supply its products according to the country's demands. Malaysia, Singapore, Caribbean and the USA require skin-off carcases while Taiwan and Korea require skin-on carcases. Some markets want *toasted* carcases.

This plant processes 50% of all Australia's goats for export. The facility currently kills up to 16,000 goats per week. In 2014, the company handled about 660,000 goats. They are aiming to process 700,000 goats in 2015.

Apart from supplying the exporter's needs, harvesting the herds of wild goats in the Australian outback bolsters the income of farmers when cattle prices are low.

A distinct advantage of Australian export goats is that they are derived from vast clean, low-risk grazing areas. Therefore, they have had limited exposure to chemicals. Australia and New Zealand have a strict system (NLIS) for the identification and tracing of animals for biosecurity, food safety, product integrity and market access.

Goat Meat Products

Western Meat Exporters provides bone-in carcases with either skin-on or skin-off, or skin-on brown (a tan-coloured carcase which results from the hair being burnt and scraped off – also marketed as *burnt goat* or *toasted*).

The bone-in products are either whole carcasses or cut '6-way', or as boneless primal cuts packed into lined cartons. All products are described and delivered in accordance with Ausmeat specifications.

While in earlier times in the Western World, rotten fruit or animal offal was thrown at condemned criminals either in the stocks or destined for the gallows that is not the case today. When a goat is slaughtered nothing is wasted.

A wide range of offal types are packaged for export including kidneys, hearts, testes, penises, stomach linings and intestines, plus whole heads. In some countries the blood, liver and lungs are used in certain dishes, while hoofs are made into soup.

In addition, the company supplies quality goat skins salted and packed on pallets ready for shipment. These are graded and exported for processing and tanning. Sizes are often large and greater than 7 ft². Medium to small skins measure 3-7ft². Colours of the feral goats are varied and attractive.

In conclusion, goat meat is the most widely consumed red meat in the world. More than 70% of the world's population eats goat meat.

Demand in Western countries is slowly increasing as diversity in population increases and individuals are tempted by the exotic cuisines brought to them in TV cooking demonstrations.

For more information about Western Meat Exporters go to:
http://www.westernexporters.com.au

Chapter 5

GOATS - promoting the commercial goatmeat industry

Goats in Utes - A way to promote the commercial goat meat industry.

Goat's meat represents lean meat and is the most eaten meat in the world.

For goat breeders, whose focus is on the commercial (meat) side of the industry, encouraging other breeder to enter the industry is not always easy. However, here's an idea that promotes the goat meat side of the industry and encourages other farmers to enter this branch of farming.

Goats in Utes (utility vehicles, trucks or trailers) was a unique event organised to promote commercial goatmeat production at a West Australian country show some years ago. It followed on from a competition – *Dogs in Utes* which attracted 700 farm vehicles – a world record for the greatest number of farm vehicles – with a working dog (sheep-dog) sitting in the back.

The idea of the competition was to encourage commercial goat farmers to display their produce (namely meat goats) showing the standard of animal that was required by the market. It was arranged as part of a Boer Goat field day.

The main category for the competition was a group of three crossbred meat goats under 12 months of age. The animals were judged on meat quality and the uniformity of the three in the group.

"Presenting an even line is one of the most important factors when producing for the meat market," said the judge who had been breeding goats for over 20 years. He was impressed with the quality and evenness of the groups but was concerned with the level of fat on a few. He advised the growers to make sure that their animals did not become fat. It is not desirable in meat animals.

"Goatmeat is uniquely lean," he said. "If the goats are fat they are not marketable. Customers wanting fat on animals will buy some other meat product."

The second judge, a Senior Research Fellow agreed that the animals were in good condition and was impressed with the degree of muscling on the goats. "Being a practical competition there is plenty of opportunity for questions to be answered." The judge, an expert on animal nutrition said he saw the *Goats in Utes* competition as an innovative educational event for new and existing breeders. "No one has a mortgage on knowledge."

He advised on balanced nutritional requirements for livestock and said some growers were promoting too much fattening in their animals. His concern was that stud breeders were over-conditioning their bucks rendering them unsuitable for working conditions.

"You need a working buck, not one that is going to melt in the paddock. Commercial producers buy sires to improve the genetic qualities of their herd. But if a buck can't deliver the sperm when required then he is no good to the industry," he said.

"This problem is particularly applicable where a *buck-effect* mating was required. The *buck-effect* is seen when a buck is introduced to a doe herd that has had no exposure to a male goat. The does all cycle between day 6 and day 11 following introduction of the buck and are served within that 5 day period."

The result is that all kids are born at the same time and will grow to a similar export size at the time required.

The animals were assessed on uniformity, condition and fat score, and conformation. Comment was made about each group with direct feedback to the grower/producer.

The judges agreed that the competition provided a novel way of judging meat animals and promoted the commercial aspect of the goat industry.

"Competition in the show ring is OK," he said, "but at the end of the day it's the commercial growers who must reap the benefits."

Prizes were offered for various categories – first prize of $250 for a group of 5-month-old, feral/Boer cross goats. The second prize of $100 for three angora/Boer crosses.

As part of the event, breeders were shown how to feel for the depth of muscle on the goats and made comment about a group of cashmere/Boer capretto kids. Running his hand across the pliable back muscle, the judge said, "You can almost feel that the meat colour on these carcases will be correct (pale)."

He was impressed with a group of feral/Boer buck kids, which at five months old fitted into the male over 25 kg category and were "very saleable".

While the event had not attracted as many goats as dogs, it gave encouragement to the commercial breeders who are the backbone of the goat meat industry but are often neglected.

Current facts from Meat and Livestock Australia:

Currently China, India and Nigeria are the largest producers and consumers of goatmeat. By comparison, Australia is a relatively small producer of goat meat, however, it is the world leader in goat meat exports.

In 2012-13 Australia exported 31,876 tonnes of goat meat mainly to the US and Taiwan. These exports were worth Au $145.8 million FOB.

Live goats were exported from Australia mainly to Malaysia, Singapore and Brunei. The dollar value of the Live Goat exports was $9.65 million in 2011-12.

- Australian goat slaughter in 2012-13 was around 1.99 million head.
- Boer goats and rangeland goats are predominately used for meat production.
- Cashmere and Angora breeds are used in fibre production.

Ref : www.mla.com.au *Meat and Livestock Australia.*

Chapter 6

From Feral Pests to Financial Gain
The West Australian Story

(Watercolour - Goats in the bush by Jill Zeck)

The state of Western Australia is vast and isolated. It's over three times the size of Texas but has a population of only 2.5 million as against Texas's 27.5 million. It includes several diverse geographical regions and apart from sheep and cattle, it has the highest number of feral goats in any state of Australia.

Feral (not wild) goats have ranged over vast tracts of Western Australia for several hundred years. From as early as the 1600s when Dutch, French and British maritime traders and adventurers set foot on the unexplored southern continent, they purposely left goats behind to provide food for any unfortunate wretches who might be shipwrecked there at a later date.

Then, in the early 1800s, the early British colonists brought dairy goats to the west. They were later spread around by miners and railway gangs who used them as a source of milk, butter, meat and leather. Some goats were intentionally released while others escaped. The result was that the goats thrived, mated and the numbers quickly multiplied until 1928 when their numbers were so great, they were declared vermin.

By 1982 there were estimated to be 1,000,000 feral goats roaming unchecked in the west. A similar situation applied in Australia's eastern states. Having easily adapted to the inhospitable, hot, harsh and dry environments of the outback, the goats had become resilient and hardy animals.

As the pastoralists extended their boundaries to graze sheep and cattle, the feral pests were trapped, poisoned or shot either from the ground or from helicopters in very costly eradication programs. Other control methods included using *Judas* goats (with radio-transmitter collars) to find hard to locate small groups in order to muster them. Those that escaped extermination were pushed deeper into the outback.

With the goat problem impossible to control yet too large to ignore, some pastoralists realized money could be made from trapping the goats and marketing them rather than shooting them and leaving the carcases to rot.

With live-sheep shipping facilities already well-established and huge livestock vehicles on the highways capable of carrying 600-800 head of livestock to the ports, and with a ready market for the meat in Asia – just across the water, a few astute farmers quietly developed a lucrative trade in goats. In the early days few outback farmers admitted that goat sales made up the biggest part of their income.

For example, one farmer had thousands of them running wild on his 350,000 acre property, competing for feed with his sheep. Seeing the potential to farm goats for the meat market staring him in the face, 6000 goats a year were mustered from several nearby properties. Once mustered, the goats were driven into a feedlot where they received supplementary feed and served the required three months behind a 2 meter fence after which time they were classed as *domesticated*. This process involved training the goats to respect plain wire electric fences in a compound. From there, they were released into a larger grazing paddock with electric fence barriers.

Installing approved fencing was the most expensive item on large pastoral holdings where fences run for hundreds of kilometres. (Currently the requirements are for a 5 line fence consisting of 2 hot and 3 cold wires.)

With a 10-year contract to supply the Sabah government with breeding does, over 20,000 live goats were supplied in the next few years until Sabah was almost self-sufficient. From there the markets were expanded to the Middle East, and Brunei – a wealthy country with its own shipping line.

Another example comes from two adjoining pastoral stations in the Goldfields region covering an area of 700,000 acres. Despite traditionally running sheep, the station manager admitted there was no money in sheep. Being thick with Mulga (a woody bush very palatable to goats), the country was ideal for goats.

Convinced of the potential, the pastoralist fenced a paddock of 170,000 acres. The 5-line fence running for 170 kilometres. The area included 13 trap yards. Starting with approximately 4500 breeding does, 140 pure South African Boer bucks were purchased to go over them.

(Tambookie Boer bucks)

Location and Transport target markets

Western Australia's geographical position and proximity to Asia are significant advantages for the live shipping trade. Live goat exports were able to *piggy-back* on the sheep-ships heading to the Middle East. Managed goats (taken from the feedlots) travel far better on the ships than pure ferals that suffer greater shipboard losses.

Apart from the live meat trade, abattoirs licenced for export and *Halal* killing provide for frozen exports. Markets in both U.S.A. and Canada consist of both skin-on and skin-off carcases which are required during the northern winter, while Australia's nearest neighbours, Malaysia and Singapore, require skin-off goats all year round. However, the biggest market by far for frozen goat meat from Western Australia is Taiwan which requires skin-on carcases weighing 14-16 kgs, the peak period being October to February.

In all cases the markets want carcases to be Class1 fat score. Overseas markets do not want fat goats.

Goat prices best ever (January 2015)

According to the Australian Broadcasting Commission, goat producers in Western Australia's rangelands are receiving the highest prices for their livestock for about 30 years. This is partially the result of unseasonal dry conditions and increased wild dog attacks, which have greatly reduced the number of feral goats roaming wild. Some farmers are receiving between $50 and $70-a-head. This represents double the prices seen in 2014.

Most of Australia's processed goat meat goes to America.

In the north of Western Australia goats are mainly processed through Geraldton Meat Exports (GME) which has been Western Australia's largest exporter of rangeland goats for more than 10 years exporting worldwide to USA, Taiwan, Malaysia, Mauritius, Vietnam, Japan, Korea, Canada, Jamaica and Trinidad.

Processing Goat meat on the other side of Australia is undertaken by Western Meat Exporters in Queensland (see Goat Meat – Chevon/Mutton)

Images of mature Boer Bucks are courtesy of the Tambookie Stud of Western Australia. Go to:
https://tambookieboergoatstud.wordpress.com.
More about GME's processing can be found at:
http://www.gmexports.com.au/

Chapter 7

Mustering goats from the Air – is like a game of chess

Flying a single-engine Cessna, this outback pilot has covered thousands of miles of territory in Western Australia rounding up goats, sheep and cattle. From the air he takes full control of the muster. Only he knows where the goats are. Flying at an altitude of 500 feet he can see the men on motor bikes and by radio contact can position them exactly where he wants them.

(Tambookie Boer Goats – Western Australia)

"It's like a game of chess," he said. With the help of six men, a goat-muster usually takes three or four days. "But it's not a simple matter of just pushing a mob along. First you have to find them then gather them together then move them in the direction you want them to go without losing any. It might sound simple, but to do this you have to know how the goat thinks," he says.

"Goats are not like a sheep (to move), they are more like cattle. A goat has a brain. A sheep hasn't. You have to convince the goat that it's his idea to move to where you want him to go.

"With goats you influence them with the noise of the aircraft, the men on bikes just hang around to make sure that none break away. Because a goat can hear a motor bike, on a still day, from six miles away, you've got to get the bikes to stay well back. You do not crowd a goat."

On the ground, the riders cannot see the mob of goats. The pilot tells them when to move and where to move to, and when to switch the bike engines off and remain silent. Bike riders sometimes ride all day without seeing another bike. Only in the last few hours of the muster do the riders and mob come together.

"You don't use the aircraft's shadow with goats," the pilot said. "Just the noise. It irritates them – like a mosquito. The knack is to irritate the goat but not harass it, just get it slightly aggravated. That makes it want to move. Once it's moving, you just keep irritating it."

Another thing is knowing the best times to muster.

"The rangeland goats mob up at certain times and disband for unknown reasons. Usually they stay in small groups of about a dozen, but twice a year they come together. Once, at a certain time in winter, when they are all in good health, they suddenly congregate in large mobs. Small groups of twelve, swell to groups of two to three hundred. Similarly, in summer, they form into huge mobs. I have seen 700 goats congregating around a watering hole," he said.

"When you find scattered groups, the technique for mustering goats is again different to sheep. With sheep you push up the little mobs and add them to the main mob.

This doesn't work with goats. The little mobs are outcasts, sometimes small individual family groups who choose to stay well away from the main mob and are reticent to join them. With the plane you pick up the big mob of goats and use it like a sponge driving those goats from one side of the range to the other, and in the process mopping up little mobs along the way. Once the mob is collected and droving, then they seem to quieten down and appear half-domesticate within a few hours," he said.

"The big bush Billys is usually no trouble. If they are introduced to new groups of goats, then they spend the whole muster trying to mate. While Billy is busy fornicating you can do what you want with his mob, so long as he is making sure there will always be a mob of goats, he is happy. We just keep them moving and they are no trouble.

"When you have collected all the groups together, you get the bikes to maintain the same distance and follow the mob into the trap yards. By the time they arrive, I have usually landed the plane and find myself on a motorbike. If you are not careful this is when you may lose some animals. A good dog can round up an escaping goat but we don't use dogs much because of the distances. It's very hard on a dog if he has to run alongside the motorbike for three days.

"Once the goats are yarded they domesticate fairly quickly but they also lose weight quickly too. You have to get them away (trucked out) as soon as possible."

From the outback the goats are loaded onto four-deck road trains for the long journey to the Geraldton abattoirs or the docks for a waiting boat. With the cost of the road-train plus six men's wages and food, and flying time, a mob of at least a 1000 goats must be shipped to make the exercise viable.

Loading goats is not always fun

"Running the goats onto the truck is usually easy and can be done in 3 to 4 hours, but I remember one occasion when this was not the case. We were loading out of Edjudina Station. We had over a thousand goats yarded. Unfortunately the crate on the truck was made of aluminium and the light was shining out of it and the goats would not go near it.

"We had worked for three days in temperatures around 100 degrees. It had been hot and thirsty weather. It was getting late in the afternoon and the boys were looking forward to a drink when we finished so we sent one of the boys to the wet-mess at the nearby Palfrey Mine to get a couple of cartons of beer.

"But the goats refused to go up the loading ramp onto the shining truck. They would not budge. By the time we pushed the last goat on, the sun was coming up the following morning, the beer was warm and we hadn't even opened one can. The six of us had to load those goats one at a time – all 1000 of them."

The pilot smiled when he remembered another time when things didn't go as planned.

Mature coloured Angora Buck

"We had just loaded the triple decker plus two trailers. The open top deck was loaded with the big Billys. This was normal because they don't fit on the lower decks with their wide spreading horns. One of the riders was a diabetic and was always swigging on a bottle of water by the loading ramp," the pilot said. "I remember this big buck looking over the top, and as Tom took the top off his water bottle, the goat jumped.

"I don't know if it wanted a drink or whatever but it landed right on Tom's shoulders.

"It broke one of the guy's legs and turned his other ankle so badly we couldn't get his boot off. I had to fly him into Kalgoorlie. He had to lay in the back of the aircraft with his feet hanging over the passenger seat just under my nose. I think he had worn these boots without socks for about a month and the stink of his feet...! I will always remember that flight.

"Old Tom didn't like goats much after that!" he said.

"I have to agree, goats can be very frustrating but there is no point in getting annoyed with them or you can't handle them."

This outback pilot logged hundreds of flying hours in his Cessna 177 high winged aircraft every season. "You can't see the ground from low winged planes. Also the high wings make it possible to taxi down laneways and through gateways."

Flying from Perth to the station country usually takes 2 to 3 hours. The plane has a range of 5.5 hours with a five-hour fuel tank. "But only two-hour seats!" he added with a sigh.

As many of the outback station are around 1,000,000 acres in size, each station has several landing strips, one near the homestead and others scattered around the property – near the camp yards, wool shed or water holes. Some landing strips are just dry clay pans. On an average muster, the plane logs about 280 knots (400 kilometers).

When he's not mustering goats, this pilot operates his own diesel workshop in a West Australian country town. But if the opportunity arises and there are goats to be mustered he closes up shop and flies out to the bush.

"If there is big mob and the market prices are right – then it's worth mustering them," he said. "Goats are the cream on the top."

Note: My thanks to Darryl Bain for sharing his story which was first published in The Goat Farmer *magazine.*

Chapter 8

Of Ghosts and Goats - From the start of large-scale goat farming in Australia's outback to where it is at today

"We fenced an area of 400,000 acres which is roughly 110 km long to 50 km wide. It takes quite a while to drive around the boundary. So far we have put in 480 kilometers of fencing."

(Tambookie Boer goats – young bucks)

One hundred years ago Kookynie was a thriving gold-rush town in the Eastern Goldfields of Western Australia. In 1907 the town had a population of well over 3,500 people, a public swimming pool, eleven hotels and it received four trains a day from Kalgoorlie.

In 2010, Kookynie was a ghost town with a population of only thirteen people. However, the area has, for decades, been populated by feral goats – thousands of them.

The combined pastoral leases of Kookynie, Melita and Jeedamya, make up a total of one and a half million acres. Across part of these combined stations, the largest commercial goat farming enterprise in Western Australia began.

Traditionally these pastoral stations ran merino sheep. And although the country is harsh and the climate unforgiving, it was well-suited to wool production. Vegetation is dominated by mulga with cotton bush and other low scrub.

For many years goats roamed the Goldfields area and were regarded as feral pests competing with the sheep for the little grazing that was available. Enforced eradication of goats through mustering or shooting was the only way to reduce their numbers. But for many years some pastoralists quietly maintained an existence from harvesting and selling the rangeland goats, though few admitted publically that goats provided them with a source of income.

With the downturn in the wool industry in the 1990s, the viability of producing wool declined but on recognizing the potential in goats that could survive and thrive in that environment, four business partners decided to farm the goats commercially.

It sounds straightforward, but it was not as simple as introducing the Boer bucks to the rangeland goats and leaving them to it. Goats have to be farmed and controlled as you would on any type of livestock.

So the first requirements were yards and fencing. To conform to Agriculture Protection Board requirements fencing, consisting of two hot wires and three cold, had to be erected around the area to confine the goats.

"We have fenced an area of 400,000 acres which is roughly 110 km long to 50 km wide," said one of the partners in 2000. "It takes quite a while to drive around the boundary. So far we have put in 480 km of fencing. The internal fencing is in a grid-like pattern dividing the area into smaller paddocks of 25,000 acres. Where four of the paddocks join, a trap yard is constructed at the water hole."

The distance between waterholes is about 15 kilometers. Here sub-artesian water is pumped from bores to the surface from a depth of about 25 meters. With low rainfall and no natural surface water, the goats must come into the trap-yards to drink. To pump the underground water, the old windmills were replaced with solar power units.

Because the land is covered in low scrub, mustering is extremely difficult by motorbike while helicopter mustering is both difficult and expensive. Trap yards are the most cost-effective way of controlling goats in this type of country.

After the feral goats were mustered, the females were drafted off to retain as base breeding stock. The bucks are trucked away on 6-deckers to either Perth airport or the docks at Fremantle 800 kilometers away.

With the numbers greatly reduced in number, more rangeland goats were bought in from other outlying stations, some coming from as far as Yalgoo – 1000 kilometers to the north-west."

At the time, orders for goats were coming in from various countries in South East Asia and each had its own market requirement. While some buyers demanded specific weights, others wanted males still entire. Some wanted white goats only. Some customers wanted all-black animals. Occasionally there were orders for feral does to be used for breeding purposes not meat.

With Melita/Kookynie station running 9000 breeding does, the partners aim was to improve the feral lines by introducing South African Boer goat genetics by using both live mating and frozen genetics to achieve this.

In 1998 they took delivery of 200 pure Boer bucks from various sources in Western Australia and South Australia to put over the rangeland goats. These sires were run at a mating rate of 4% because of the distances the animals covered. Since then a major program has been embarked on with frozen embryos to increase the pool of genetic material.

While both programs have proved successful some problems arose that had not been anticipated.

South African Boer bucks are big animals with a docile temperament particularly if raised on a quarantine station or stud farm. By comparison, however, the size and aggressive nature of the male feral goats running in the station country is amazing.

Some of the full grown bucks weigh 150 kgs. They are so big they intimidated the Boer bucks forcing them to congregate on their own away from the herd.

The dominant rangeland bucks, with wide a span of horns, have been known to rip open the testicles of the young Boer sires rendering them infertile. The short horns of the Boer bucks are no match for them.

Fencing was a problem in the early years.

"The wild feral bucks would either jump the fences or come straight through the electric wires. Despite being zapped, they would push through and once in the paddock they would head straight for the does. It appeared that the fences were not only keeping the domesticated goats in but allowing the ferals in to join them."

To keep the aggressive bush Billys away from the does at mating time, the does were brought into smaller areas for mating with the pure Boers. The mating yard consists of a 200-acre paddock constructed with mesh fencing around. About 500 does were introduced at a time after being scanned for pregnancy. Does that were found to be pregnant to the rangeland bucks had their pregnancy terminated.

In those early years, the rangeland goats domesticated quickly in the training yards. They soon got used to the electric fencing and to people – the station being run by a manager and 3 stockmen – and the newly introduced Boer genetics quickly improved the meat quality, quantity and temperament of the rangeland ferals.

(Tambookie Boer Goa Stud)

2015 - Sequel to the Melita Station story

Only a few years after the introduction of the Boers on the pastoral stations of the Goldfields, a large agricultural company, running 95,000 head of cattle plus sheep in Western Australia, took up the Melita operation along with several other large scale pastoral station enterprises in the north of Western Australia. This company is **Yeeda**.

Today, Yeeda runs a 5,000 herd of goats on properties that include Melita, Jeedamya, and Kookynie Stations. The herd consist of both rangeland and Boer goats. *Yeeda* continues to introduce higher quality genetics in order to produce a heavier and higher meat quality animal. Boers and Boer crosses breed throughout the year reaching sexual maturity at 5 months of age. Multiple births are common and a 200% kid drop is achievable in managed herds.

Overview:

January 2015 - Goat producers in Western Australia's rangelands received the highest prices for their goats for about 30 years. This was due to the reduced number of animals available. Supplies had been reduced by wild dog attacks and also climatic conditions (drought) throughout the rangelands. Goats are now selling for between $50 and $70 per head – double the price achieved a year earlier.

One abattoir manager said he could not get enough goats to meet his orders. He said the industry was receiving its greatest demand which came from America, followed by Malaysia, Taiwan and smaller markets in Mauritius and the West Indies.

Most Australian goat meat, however, is exported to North America where it is the red meat preferred by Latin Americans.

2015: the Year of the Goat

(Tambookie Boer goats)

According to Chinese astrology, February 19th heralded the Year of the Goat. It also saw a time of increased interest from China in rangeland goats.

Following a visit in 2014 from the Chinese Consul and his delegation, it is obvious they want to get their hands on as many goats as possible.

Recently, the amount of Australian goat meat exported to China has skyrocketed. In 2012, China imported 500-tonnes of Australian goat meat. A year later the trade was had increased to 5000-tonnes.

It appears that business is booming for the goat meat industry in the north of Western Australia.

2015 information on Yeeda is from their website www.yeeda.com.au
The January 2015 update is from: www.abc.net.au (Australian Broadcasting Corporation).
For information about Tambookie Boer Goat Stud visit:
https://tambookieboergoatstud.wordpress.com/ *or follow them on Facebook.*

Chapter 9

MOHAIR - The *Diamond Fibre* – grown on the farm

Mohair is a luxury animal fibre produced by an Angora goat (not to be confused with angora fur from an Angora rabbit). Technically it is neither hair nor wool but a fibre that is extremely strong and durable and said to be stronger then steel (diameter for diameter). It is almost non-flammable and is claimed to be one of the most durable animal fibres there is.

Fine mohair, averaging 22 microns in diameter, is used commercially in the production of light-weight worsted cloth. The stronger fibres are used for knitting wools and the strongest for carpets and upholstery materials.

Why is it called the *diamond fibre*?

Mohair is called the *diamond fibre* because of its natural lustre. The closed-scale formation on each fibre acts like the facets of a diamond in reflecting light. By comparison wool, which is often medullated or hollow, appears dull. Apart from the luxury sheen, mohair has a soft handle and feels smooth and silky to touch.

One of the prime qualities of natural white mohair is its unequalled affinity to accept synthetic dyes to produce a kaleidoscope of brilliant vibrant colours which will not fade.

Quality – style and character

The finest quality mohair (the thickness of each fibre measured by its micron diameter) is shorn from kids, but as the animals mature, the fleece and fibre diameter strengthen (broaden). Cashmere is finer than mohair, but mohair is mainly finer than wool.

Mohair grows from the goat's skin in individual staples which fall in long wavy ringlets. These staples demonstrate style and character. When the ringlets have lots of twist or spirals they are described as being stylish. Character is the name given to the natural crimp, wave or corrugation which occurs in each staple. A balance between the two is desirable. The Angora's fleece covers a well-bred goat from head to tail.

Growth rate:

Mohair grows at a rate of about 100-150 mm (4-6 inches) in 6 months and is shorn twice a year. When it grows longer it has a tendency to attract burr or other vegetable contaminants from the paddock, or to become extremely tangled. It is not easy for breeders to keep their animals' fleeces in good condition when it is overlong.

Why farmers run Angora Goats commercially

Obviously, for a farmer, the reason for growing the fibre is to make as much money from each clip (shearing) as possible. But volume is not the only factor that determines what the return will be.

Like sheep's wool, mohair prices have always been cyclical as they are dependent on the demand from the cloth manufacturers in Britain and Europe. It is here that the mills blend mohair with wool to produce expensive luxury cloth which displays the distinctive mohair sheen.

Mohair fibre and Angora goat skins are also in demand in the craft industry for spinning, weaving, also for making Teddy bears and doll's wigs.

MOHAIR – from the goat's back to the cat-walks of Europe

Men's suiting fabric containing mohair has a distinctive sheen which makes it easily identifiable when worn in any board room or paraded on a male-fashion cat-walk. Manufactured in Italy or Britain, mohair fabric not only looks expensive but carries an appropriate price-tag. It is associated with high-end customers who only put their names to top quality fabrics such as Louis Vuitton and Armani, Polo Ralph Lauren, J Crew, and Gucci.

The company, *Safil* of Italy, owns the largest single worsted spinning mill in Europe making a wide range of high quality yarns and fabrics in wool and wool blends including mohair. It is located in Plovdiv (Bulgaria) and produces 7000 tons a year. Of the 300 tonnes of mohair and mohair-blended yarns that are processed there, 80% of the fibre is sourced from South Africa.

Cesare Savio, the owner of *Safil*, said that presently the majority of mohair is used for knitwear and hand knitting yarns, which is in keeping with most people's image of the fibre's end-product. But the luxury characteristics of mohair have long been recognized by the industry as ideally suited to apparel and other fabric uses.

While fine quality tailored suiting is made from mohair blended with wool or other natural fibres, Mr Savio believed there is a market for pure mohair Italian suits.

Unlike wool, mohair is a niche fibre as there are only a few million kilograms produced worldwide. South Africa produces about 4,000,000 kilos annually, of which only about 100,000 kg would meet the requirements of fabric weaving sector.

Australia exports about 130,000 kg of mohair per year (Dec 2013) and is now growing some of the finest mohair in the world. Encouraged by Italy's biggest spinner, current trial are being undertaken to further improve the fibre's quality and length.

In the mill –raw fibre transformed into fine yarn

Several years ago I visited Britain and was privileged to be shown through two mohair processing mills. Since that time both mills have closed their old premises.

The first was a traditional 19th century Yorkshire mill building of 7-8 storeys high. After trudging up the stone steps to the top floor, I watched as bales of mohair were opened and the fibre reclassed by a dozen workers. The stencils on the sides of the bales indicated they came from South Africa, Texas, Lesotho, Argentina, Turkey and Australia. The Turkish fibre appeared course, kempy and very greasy. I learned that the angoras were only shorn once a year due to the climatic conditions – the mohair was between 8 and 12 inches in length.

South African mohair is regarded most highly, but today South African genetics are not limited to that country's goats.

From the classing area, the fibre was sent to the scouring, carding and combing mill some distance away. I next visited the spinning mill where the mohair is spun into tops and then mixed with varying percentages of other natural or man-made fibres and lightly spun onto rovings. These rovings are then spun down to 100 times finer thread.

The mill made yarn for various products including high quality mohair velour. Most of the velour was exported to a toy manufacturer in Germany for making expensive teddy bears. Top quality mohair velour is also used for plush furnishings in top cruise liners and first class European hotels.

The second mill I visited was John Forster and Son's Black Dyke Mill, established in 1817. It was the largest vertically integrated spinning and weaving mill in Yorkshire that had been producing world famous quality worsted and worsted/mohair apparel fabrics for almost 200 years.

The selvedge edge of the cloth carried such labels as: *Celine Paris 60% Summer Kid Mohair and Worsted, Givenchy Gentlemen Paris,* and *Dunhill Ltd–60% Summer Kid Mohair.* Fabrics were woven using blends of wool, mohair, cashmere, silk and linen.

Almost as famous as the Yorkshire mill is the Black Dyke Band, formerly John Foster & Son Black Dyke Mill Band. It is one of the oldest and best-known brass bands in the world. In 2014, the band won the National Brass Band Championship of Great Britain for a record 23rd time.

Chapter 10

GOATS - A Colour Kaleidoscope - Coloured Angoras

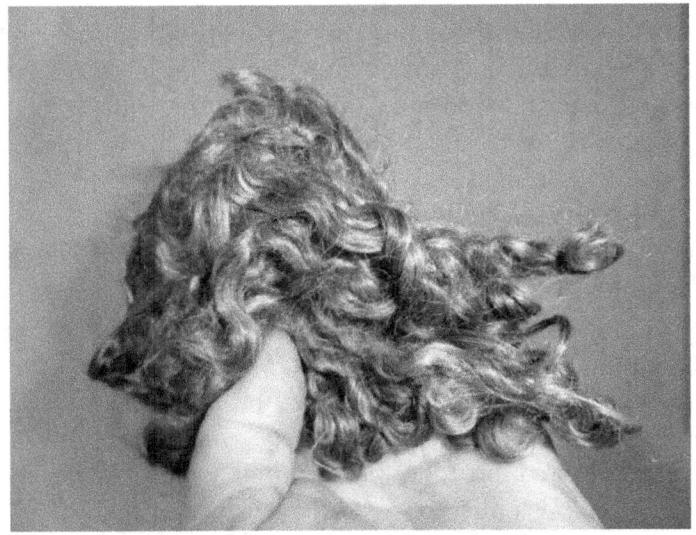

Lustrous Australian coloured mohair

One of the prime qualities of mohair is its ability to accept synthetic dyes and produce vibrant colours. However, if you are a handspinner or weaver, the warm subtle grey or brown tones produced by naturally coloured Angora goats are a delight to behold.

Smokey grey, silver, charcoal even rich brown and ginger, and more rarely, apricot are all available, and if you want to experiment with synthetic dyes over these, the resulting hues are amazingly rich and warm. For breeders of coloured Angoras, white is the dominant colour gene, grey is second whereas brown and apricot are recessive and more difficult to achieve.

It is not only the *colour gene* that makes these Angoras different. The inside of the skin of a culled animal is sky blue and if held up to the light is very dense as against the skin of a white Angora. In some Asian countries a premium price is paid for these blue skinned goats.

Apart from the fibre shorn from these attractive animals, staples of coloured fleece can be used for dolls' wigs or felting. Tanned skins (I used the Leidreiter's Tanning method) are used to make naturally coloured teddy bears or floor rugs, and the goats themselves make an interesting tourist attraction.

Coloured Angoras are naturally good mothers and often mate earlier in the season and twin more often than their white counterparts – perhaps due to being less inbred and closer to feral stock from which the line was developed.

However, breeders who run coloured Angoras together with white animals must follow certain protocols to ensure the white fleece does not become contaminated with coloured fibres or that a white goat is not carrying the black gene (from an unplanned mating).

Shearing of black/coloured goats should be performed separately from the white flock – preferably on a different day as you would if running coloured sheep along with whites. Also if possible – run your coloured animals in a separate paddock, even then fibre contamination can occur from animals rubbing on wire fences. Care and observation are prerequisites in fleece preparation.

For the coloured breeder, kids should be tagged at birth and unwanted male kids culled or castrated at one week old. Don't forget that white kids born of black mothers will carry a black recessive gene.

Breeding coloured Angoras provides some of the breeding challenges that mohair growers experienced before the importation of new genetics from South Africa and Texas in the late 1990s - namely a desire to increase yields without forfeiting micron fineness and lustre.

For breeders of coloured flocks, kidding time is particularly delightful and exciting.

What colour kids will the doe produce?

Most coloured kids are born with a jet black fleece which is short, coarse and very curly. As the coloured kid grows, true mohair replaces the kid fibre and the grey fleece may appear ginger on the tips. But the tinged ends will disappear as the fibre grows into a true shade of grey.

Well before the infamous book *Fifty shades of Grey* was published, I marketed my coloured mohair under the name *Shades of Grey Mohair*.

Skins from aborted or culled newborn black kids have the properties of astrakhan. For makers of dolls' wigs, these skins are very desirable for boy-dolls – the shaped pate being cut from a tanned kid skin and stuck directly onto the doll's head.

Imported lines of improved genetics were introduced into white flocks almost 20 years ago (in Australia) to produce heavier and denser fleeces. However, though fleece production can be improved, some breeders of coloured animals do not want to depart from the silky soft and extremely fine micron fibre size of the diamond fibre that the coloured Angora carries.

The natural coloured fleece is highly sought after by hand-spinners and weavers and can be used virtually straight from the goat's back. Though slippery due to its silkiness, it is a delight to spin on its own but is even better when blended with alpaca or fine wool, silk or other natural fibre. It produces a soft, silky luxury yarn.

Just like white Angoras, the goats need shearing twice a year (unless you want to grow a particularly long coloured fleece suitable for a doll's wig). This speciality product will return a premium price.

As a hobby farmer or tourist park operator, if you only want to run a handful of goats, the smaller framed, docile coloured Angora is a delightful choice and, while black fibre cannot be sold in commercial quantities, crafts people will welcome your product as it is a sheer delight to spin.

Some agricultural shows have special competition categories for both coloured animals and their fleeces. Pens of live animals always attract a lot of attention.

Why not let Coloured Angoras colour your world?

Note: Several years ago the author ran a flock of 20 coloured Angoras in Western Australia along with 150 white mohair goats. She has spun coloured mohair and also made teddy bears, soft toys and floor rugs from home-tanned skins.

Chapter 11

MOHAIR - Fibre for Craft – Spinning and Weaving, Dolls' wigs and skins for Teddy Bears

Spinning and Weaving

(Coloured mohair dyed and spun: MM)

Because of its silky nature and the absence of hooklets on each fibre (as found on wool fibres), mohair slides very easily and is not an easy fibre for beginners to spin. However, once you are used to handling it, you will fall in love with the feel of it.

As a spun yarn it has a beautiful lustre that will accept synthetic dyes and produce brilliant lasting colours. Blending mohair and wool together makes spinning easier though some of the mohair's brilliant lustre will be lost in the spun yarn.

Naturally coloured mohair is always in demand from hand spinners.

Making felt from mohair is very difficult because, unlike wool, it lacks the hooklets which makes the fibres cling to each other. However, by blending wool and mohair together felting is possible and the results can be amazing.

Dolls' wigs

For centuries, doll makers have used mohair to create flowing ringlets for their dolls' hair. With its soft handle, beautiful lustre, natural curl, and ability to accept both natural and synthetic dyes, mohair is the traditional fibre for making luxury wefts.

Large dolls require wefts made from mohair up the 30 cm (12 inches) in length.

(Mohair wig- photos:MM)

Wig wefts

Wefted mohair is made by sewing pieces of shorn fleece along a length of tape or special soluble adhesive strip. Staples of fibre are hand-picked for length and quality-consistency and machined to the strip or binding. Once the hair is secured, the weft can be washed gently and dyed using human hair dyes or synthetics.

Approximately 1m to 1.5m is required to fit a large doll. This is sewn in circles onto a mesh on the doll's head.

Wigs vary in length from a little over a centimetre in length, on a small boy doll's head, up to 30cm on the large French fashion dolls.

Whatever the choice, be it white or black, long or short, colour-dyed or natural, a mohair wig will provide a doll of any size with its crowning glory – a beautiful head of lustrous curls.

A breeder's story

For several years, one Australian stud breeder handcrafted lengths of wefted mohair and sold these to doll-makers at home and overseas.

The producer had been involved in breeding Angora goats for twenty-five years. During this time she had classed most of the stud's mohair clip and selected the best fleeces for competitions. Because the stud ran a large number of goats, there were plenty to choose from.

The best mohair producing Angoras are selected from those carrying free flowing blocky staples. Dry and fine mohair is more likely to develop crossed fibres as the hair grows.

"Some style (the twisted ringlet) and character (the crimp or waviness of each lock) are important but if it has too much of either, it is not suitable for wig wefts."

To achieve the extra length required for wig making, suitable angoras are selected when they are carrying a six month fleece. From then on, the goats are kept in the farm shed for a further six months, housed on a raised mesh floor and only allowed out to graze on short grass in good weather.

This is necessary to avoid vegetable matter contaminating the fleece. During the second six months the goats are given a wash or dip. Despite being shedded the breeder was surprised how dirty the fleece became.

When preparing the wefts, the producer works with the shorn-end of the mohair. She hand picks each staple and machines it into a long weft over a meter in length. The wefts are then washed and dyed.

Craftspeople want short hair for baby dolls. Kid fleece is popular for fairy dolls as it offers ultra-soft fly-away hair with a nice lustre.

Some doll-makers want hair on tanned skin in order to cut a round pate which can be glued to a porcelain head. The skin of unwanted new-born soot-black kids with tight curly astrakhan-like curls is in great demand for boys' wigs.

Long white mohair is in demand in December for Father Christmas' beards. The various demands of wig-makers are constant.

Tanned Angora goats skins

No farmer wants to retain a lot of young bucks therefore the male kids are usually killed for the table or sold for meat. Capretto, or kid goat, is a healthy and popular gastronomic commodity.

Tanned skins with hair-on from young or old animals have their uses. They make attractive scatter rugs.

Coloured goat skins in their natural shades are also ideal for making grey or brown teddy bears and other soft toys. And for anyone prepared to experiment with synthetic dyes on natural grey fleeces, the resulting colours are amazingly rich and warm.

MOHAIR production – use of TEASELS

The teasel, teazel or teazle is a flowering plant (considered an invasive species in the USA). It is native to Europe, Asia and northern Africa and grows to 1–2.5 metres (3.3–8.2 feet).

For hundreds of years teasels were used to create the fluffy finish for which mohair is recognized. Evidence exists that teasels were used to comb the mohair cloth worn by the Pharaohs of Egypt.

Historically, teasels were used as a natural comb for cleaning, aligning and raising the *nap* (downy finish) on wool or mohair.

With their prickly stem and leaves, and purple, dark pink or lavender coloured flowers, teasels are easily identified.

In textile manufacturing, the dried flower heads were attached to spindles, wheels, or cylinders, sometimes called teasel frames, to tease the fibres in the fabric. One problem with teasel heads in commercial production was that they wore out very quickly so, by the 20th century, teasels were replaced with metal hand-cards or small brushes.

Craft workers, however, who hand-spin, knit or weave cloth at home often prefer to use dried teasels when finishing their fabric.

Chapter 12

Goat dairy meets the demand for gourmet Goat's Milk Cheese

If you have sailed on a Cunard cruise liner or flown Qantas out of Australia, it is likely that you have been served Kytren French-style goat's milk cheese. Margaret and Ken Vinicombe started making gourmet cheese on their Morangup property in 1996 and soon received numerous prestigious awards.

The Vinicombes believe their gourmet produce has helped change the old attitude toward goats especially amongst the younger generation.

"Gourmet cheese is a growing market with more people turning towards goat products," Margaret said.

For six years prior to starting their own goat business both Ken and Margaret worked for another goat dairy and saw the huge potential in the industry and also noted where improvements could be made. Even in the early days, demand outweighed supply.

With this in mind, the couple bought a complete dairy herd consisting of 40 milking does and two bucks and Ken built a dairy on their 10.5 ha (25 acre) hills property. Apart from the sheds, dairy and cool room, he constructed special feeders for grain and hay. Originally the goats included Saanen and Saanen-crosses with a few Toggenburgs, British Alpines and Anglo Nubians but because the Toggenburgs tended to overeat with *ad lib* feeding, the Saanens became the established breed.

With natural mating and breeding programs, the herd increased and today, after 19 years in business, the flock consists of 180 milking does, 30 dry does and 40 kids.

In the purpose built dairy, with nine milking bails, the nannies produce from 5-6 litres per day. Ken culls heavily for low milk production unless the doe is in its first lactation. From the onset he used the New Zealand's *Tru Test* milk meter and still monitors production four or 5 times a year. By this method, he is able to chart total herd performance also individual goat production quantities.

From each 10 litre bucket of milk Margaret makes 14 round cheeses each weighing about 140 grams. Each day about 25-30 kg of cheese is produced. The award-winning, French-style farmhouse cheeses are marketed under the label *Kytren - Pure Goat's Milk Cheese*. Made with 100% goat's milk very little else is added apart from salt, oil and herbs in some of the varieties.

The dairy makes seven types including soft-curd and white-mould cheeses, which are firmer, and a small medallion cheese which is put into oil and coated with pepper and garlic.

Cheeses are made in two sizes and four flavours including plain, herb, pepper and ash-coated. Ash, when used as a preservative, gives a cheese a nutty flavour.

Originally most of the Kytren cheeses were freshly wrapped, however, vacuum packing has extended the shelf-life of each cheese to seven weeks.

Apart from cheese, today the farm also produces milk and drinking yoghurt. This relatively new dairy product is a creamy healthy drink packed with nutrients. Kytren produces one of the few dinking yoghurts made from goat's milk.

Raising a dairy herd

The goats are fed on pellets and hay and have access to seasonal grass in the paddocks. They also have access to ground salt, mineral lick blocks and dolomite. Ken has not encountered many health problems in the flock and attributes that to good feed and hygiene. His husbandry includes 3 in 1 vaccine, Cobalt and Selenium pellets, lice treatment and twice yearly drenches.

"Our overheads include feed and minimal vet bills. We don't call the vet unless it is compulsory," said Ken.

An early Embryo Transfer program yielded a poor result, however, an Artificial Insemination program was successful. Hormone controlled mating has been used to ensure a flush of kids are dropped together. This results in a flush of milk. The nannies kid naturally in the paddocks and doe kids are retained to increase stock numbers. The goats normally drop their kids in August and September and are kept in milk for 18 months or two years.

Following every milking, the goats' teats are submerged in an antibacterial solution which kills germs and adds lanolin to prevent chaffing. Despite the twice daily milking, Ken has not encountered problems with udders or mastitis. He prefers to use a teat dip rather than an antibacterial mist spray which some dairy farmers recommend. "As you only spray from one side you can miss the orifice."

Running the farm and dairy is a seven day a week job. Milking takes about one hour morning and afternoon with half an hour for preparation and cleaning up afterwards. Freshly packed cheeses are delivered to local producers twice a week and interstate orders are delivered to Perth airport twice a week.

"Attitudes are changing," said Margaret. Today, with the growing popularity of cooking programs on TV and a more healthy-eating mentality, interest in gourmet products including goat cheese is expanding. "Because the fat content is a lot less than in regular cow cheese, people who want to eat cheese and increase their calcium intake prefer the goat product. People who are lactose intolerant can eat goat's cheese without adverse effects," she said.

The Vinicombes attribute their success to aggressive marketing, attention to herd health and hygiene, and a commitment to succeeding in the goat industry.

Margaret admits that dairying is a demanding business with twice a day milking, seven days a week plus the time devoted to cheese making and to the animals, but after 23 years in the business she is proud of the Kytren Goat Dairy and the cheeses she produces.

Note: *The Kytren Goat Dairy is located in Western Australia. I first visited the farm and interviewed Margaret Vinicombe several years ago. My thanks to Margaret for providing an update. Photos appear in the e-book version of this book.*

Chapter 13

This farm on wheels brings goat kids to city kids

You have probably heard the English ditty - *Old MacDonald had a farm e-i-e-e-o.*
But have you heard of *Old Macdonald's Travelling Farms?*

The Old Macdonald's team at a pit-stop

While the colourful mobile trailers transport a host of small farm animals across Australia, the main attraction is always the goat kids. With their delightful antics, individual personalities and friendly nature they prove most popular with audiences of any age. "Goats are ideal because they are so adaptable," the Farm operator said.

In Australia the Travelling Farms operate on a franchise basis in each state. To go on the road, each operator is equipped with a brightly painted horse float packed with tents, barriers and 40 assorted young animals. Travelling together with a variety of goat kids, which are the most popular, are lambs, piglets, rabbits, ducks, chickens and even a calf.

"You can imagine the looks we get when people see the colourful float at road rest stops. From the number of people who stop to take photos it is obvious even the vehicle is a tourist attraction!"

For the animals of the travelling farm, the extended horse float is their farm-shed on wheels. And it is often their home for several weeks. On one country trip, the West Australian troupe travelled 5,500 kilometers.

At each location the operators set up a large enclosure with portable barriers and a decorated green tent. Once the animals have settled in, the public are allowed in to hand-feed, touch and mingle with the babies.

The main venues are schools and kindergartens, country fairs and agricultural shows, shopping centres and nursing homes. It often surprises the operators how many country bookings they get for their farm animals.

But the role is not simply entertainment.

Old Macdonald's Farms are approved by the Department of Education as an educational unit for primary children. At schools they promote the attributes of the goats for meat, fibre and milk production. At fairs and shows they explain about goat milk and use of fibre for spinning and weaving.

The question most frequently asked is "What's that?" and it usually refers to an angora kid. "Angoras confuse everyone. Surprisingly many adults and teachers think fibre goats are sheep or lambs." It seems that most people identify goats by their smooth hair and horns.

Travelling with the animals, the operators recognize the different characteristics of the various breeds at an early age.

"The dairy goats are the attention seekers. They like to be around you and be next to you. I think the Saanans and Alpines are the most loving and the friendliest.

"They are the ones the children often prefer. The Anglo Nubians kids are more striking with their multi-coloured markings, but they are rather like spoilt children and often have a mind of their own.

(Feral kid – R. Dunn – NZ)

"The nursery also includes feral kids. These also are pretty often in mixed colours and are far more independent than the dairy breeds. They think barriers are made for jumping over," the operator said. "They are our Houdinis. And the angora kids are the timid ones." Both white and black angoras travel with the troupe.

And what about the Boer goat kids?

(Boer goat kids - MM)

"We have a team of nine Boers and Boer crosses at the moment," I was told. "They are like nine rugby union players in a pack. They always have to be first out of the float and first fed. You can hear their feet clopping along behind you like baby elephants."

I asked if there was a difference between the behavior of the kids and lambs and was told that the goat kids want attention, whereas the lambs don't seem to need human contact.

"Kids that join the troupe at a few days old need no training and go straight on the road but lambs take a little longer to settle in."

Feeding times are popular with any audience. The kids are fed three bottles of cold formula daily. Children love to help. At a fair in a capital city recently 1000 children visited the mobile farmyard. At the shows, *Old Macdonald's Travelling Farms* charges a small entry fee. For an extra fifty cents children can buy a cup of feed for the animals.

At the end of the day the tent and barriers are dismantled and the animals returned to their mobile farm shed to sleep. "The different breeds interact extremely well. They are one big happy cross-species family."

The operators source their animals from local breeders and are happy to receive orphaned kids and unwanted males. The kids stay with them from three to six months depending on their nature and rate of growth and when they graduate there is no problems finding good homes for them.

For the Travelling Farms operators life is hectic, but also rewarding in more ways than one. "The smiles make it all worthwhile."

"And it's not only children who derive pleasure from the farm. Adults who are passing often stop to look over our barriers. Their faces light up when they see the children surrounded by animals. The animals are so calm they seem to have a calming effect on everyone."

Plus, the constant stream of questions confirms that *Old Macdonald's* is not just an entertainment unit. "We make every attempt to educate the public and feel strongly that this is one of our roles as a travelling animal farm."

Note: For information on the Old Macdonald's Travelling Farms go to:
http://www.oldmacfarms.com.au/

Chapter 14

The Bagot Goat – its history spanning 800 years

Swiss Mountain Goats from Bigstock Photos

If ever a goat was an enigma, it is the Bagot Goat. It is neither a fibre goat nor a meat goat. It is, in fact, a rare breed species which, against all odds, has survived the centuries.

Here is its heartwarming story:

The history of the Bagot goat is interlaced with images of knights on horseback, Kings and coats of arms, a story spanning 800 years where fact, legend and folklore are closely intertwined.

This rare and ancient breed, probably England's oldest, survived for centuries under the protection of one aristocratic family. But later, because the breed was deemed to be of little intrinsic value, attempts were made to exterminate it.

By 1979 only 12 goats remained in the herd. Had it not been for the help of a dedicated group of enthusiasts the pure Bagot goat could have been lost forever.

When Richard the Lionheart returned from the Holy Land in 1194, the evil Prince John was Regent of England and Robin Hood and his Merry Men championed the poor from Sherwood Forest. This legend is well known. But almost unknown is the story that when Richard returned from the Crusades he brought back a few black headed goats from the Rhone Valley of Switzerland.

Two hundred years later, in 1380, a young King Richard the Second presented the herd of black and white goats to Sir John Bagot at Blithfield Hall in Staffordshire. These were released into Bagots Park, 800 acres of woodland on the edge of the great Needlewood Forest. Here beneath the majestic oaks the goats ran freely. With the Lord's wild deer, they provided sport for the royal hunting parties and Bagot's Park was their home for 600 years.

For centuries legend and folklore allowed the black-headed goat to live a protected life. One story tells that long ago a poacher killed a Bagot goat and ate it. Immediately, he became very ill with a mysterious illness. After that the goats were untouched despite the poachers still stealing the Lord's deer.

Unlike deer, by law, the goats were not classed as wild but, if the goats strayed onto local farmland, the Estate had to pay for any damage to the crops. It is said that the farmers may have encouraged the goats to escape onto their land in order to claim compensation.

In 1380, Sir John Bagot incorporated a goat's head into the Bagot coat of arms. It became the family's mascot. Sir John's helmet, which rests in the Blithfield Church, has a goat's head on the top of it. And displayed at Blithfield Hall is a magnificent set of goat horns that measure almost 4 feet across.

But the legend, which closely unites the goats with the Bagot family from which they take their name, is that if ever the Bagot goat dies out, the House of Bagot will fall. This belief possibly ensured the survival of the breed.

Over the years the size of the herd fluctuated. As numbers increased some culling was done. In 1920 and 1954 a few Bagot bucks were sent to the Rhinog Mountains in Wales. Today some of the wild goats of the Rhinog have distinctive Bagot markings.

But in 1939 it appeared that the fate of the Bagot herd was sealed. The Staffordshire Water Authority bought the Blithfield Estate. They planned to flood the old forest and grazing land to create a massive reservoir. Because the Bagot goat was considered to be of no commercial value, it was to be exterminated.

Fortunately, with the outbreak of the Second World War construction of the reservoir was postponed but, the following year, the War Agriculture Executive issued the extermination order. Lord Bagot disputed this and the goats were given a reprieve, but the Court stipulated that the herd must not exceed sixty head.

At the end of the war, work on the reservoir resumed and in 1953 most of the land was flooded and the remaining forest was cleared for farming. The Water Authority had allowed the 5th Lord Bagot to continue living in Blithfield Hall but the stately home had fallen into disrepair. When he died, the 6th Lord and his wife, Australian born, Nancy Lady Bagot decided to buy it back together with some of the surrounding land. After considerable expense and extensive restoration, Blithfield Hall was opened to the public in 1956.

Of the hundred goats which had roamed the woodland, only twenty were kept. These were brought to the Hall by Lady Bagot. The remaining wild goats were caught and sold. A few went to private farms or zoos, others were killed. A group was sent to Hal Bagot, in Cumbria.

But the goats at Blithfield Hall were destined to live in a walled garden and small paddock near the house. Gone was the natural environment of the primeval forest. Their survival was in doubt and by 1979 only 12 goats remained. This gave the Bagot breed the dubious distinction of being, not only on the critical list of British endangered breeds, but featuring as the rarest of the rare breeds by the British Rare Breeds Survival Trust (RBST).

Nancy Lady Bagot felt she had no option but to entrust the remaining animals to the RBST in a hope that they would ensure the survival of the breed. Perhaps the old legend prompted her do this.

The Trust decided that the only way to protect the species was to increase their numbers as quickly as possible they embarked on a grading-up program using base stock of various breeds and crossing them with pure Bagots. After four crosses the goat was classed as pedigree. But a handful of enthusiasts could see that the true bloodline of the ancient breed was in danger of being lost.

The Bagot Goat Breeders Study Group was formed in 1987. Their aim was to promote the breed and maintain its integrity. Their approach was different to that taken by the Trust.

Over the previous 80 years culled animals had been relocated around England and Wales. It was to these sources of pure lines that the Bagot Study Group directed their attention. By tracing the history of the animals and selecting from the small closed herds, a breed register of pure stock was compiled.

In 1979 the Group converted to a full Breed Society affiliated to the British Goat Society. Today, thanks to the efforts of those enthusiasts, there are hundreds of registered Bagot goats. The secretary of the breed society said he doubted the Bagot goat would ever come close to extinction again.

Although there are no Bagot goats at Blithfield Hall today, a few years ago, Nancy Lady Bagot wrote, "I count myself very privileged to have known Bagots Park and to have seen the goats in their natural surroundings. It is very heartening that so many goat lovers are caring for these unique and historic animals."

Nancy Lady Bagot was President of the Bagot Goat Breed Society. She died, aged 94, in 2014.

Seeking the truth behind the legend

The story that the Bagot goat was brought to England from Switzerland hundreds of years ago, is not hard to believe when you consider the rare breeds which still roam the Alpine regions of Switzerland, Germany and Italy.

The goats, which arrived at the time of the Crusades and came to be knows as Bagot goats, probably come from the Alps of southern Switzerland, north Italy and Austria.

You only have to look at a Swiss Schwartzhal (Blacknecked or Wallis goat – pics on the www) of the Rhone Valley to recognize the colour markings and the horn structure to be convinced these animals were the likely source of the goats associated with King Richard.

To this day, black and white goats are found in the mountains of Switzerland, Italy, Austria and Germany.

The Valais Blackneck is found in the region of Valais, in southern Switzerland, and neighbouring areas of northern Italy. The largest concentration is in the area of Visp (Viège). At the end of 2013 the total numbers of goats of this type were a little over 3000 in Switzerland, with a few hundred in Italy plus only 100–300 head in Germany).

The Valais Blackneck is distinctively almost half black and half white. It is known by various names according to where it lives. In Germany it is the Walliser Schwarzhalsziege or Gletschergeiss; in France, Col Noir du Valais, Chèvre des Glaciers or Race de Viège; and in Italy, Vallesana or Vallese.

Post script

When I visited England, from Australia, several years ago, I happened across a handsome Bagot buck on a farm in the south and noted in my diary: "What a magnificent animal."

If I lived in England I would like to raise these rare breed goats. It was not until later that I discovered just how rare they were.

In 2014, I wrote a Young Adult fiction short story titled "King Richard and the Mountain Goat". *It was inspired by the Bagot Goat's story and is available from Amazon in both paperback and e-book.*

Note: Images of various black and white breeds and goats at Blithfield Hall can be seen on the Amazon Kindle version of this book.

Chapter 15

Promotion and marketing - the keys to success for breeders

It doesn't matter is you are an individual goat grower, a member of a breed society or a hobby farmer, to be successful means making yourself known and being competitive. Small and large businesses fail if they cannot promote and market their products.

Rural enterprises are no different and farmers must learn to approach their businesses in a professional manner. With the ongoing cost of feed, veterinary care, transport, fencing, stock and breeding programs, few can afford the luxury of failure.

The key to success in marketing is promotion and publicity, and many of the steps to achieving positive results are simple and inexpensive.

Firstly you must believe in your product, and secondly you must promote it and yourself in as many ways as possible. A lot can be achieved at little or no cost whatsoever.

Here are a few suggestions for promoting your livestock enterprise.

1. *Know your product.*
Improve your knowledge about the industry through reading and networking. Know your product inside out so you can answer the 1001 question people might ask.

There are lots of books available that are easily accessed from Amazon or your local bookshop. An internet search will provide lots of information. Read all you can, not only in journals and rural magazines but read other breeders' advertisements so you know what the competition is.

(Image: MM)

To be known and remembered in today's cyber-savvy world, you need a presence on the Internet. Start with a website or blog. Update your posts regularly. Be active on social media. Visit on-line groups on Facebook and join in conversations. Know the current sales prices for stud stock and fibre (mohair growers), frozen meat prices and the market trends and latest developments in your industry at home and overseas.

2. *Present a professional image.*

You are your farm's best promotional tool. Word of mouth is the cheapest form of promotion. Get to know the people involved in your industry. Find out where they are located and what they are achieving. Take time to talk on the phone, on email, or pay a visit. This is networking. Avoid being negative. Be honest and positive. Make sure you and your animals also look happy and healthy.

Suggest to new buyers to visit other enterprises to compare stock. Customers appreciate an open minded approach.

Be professional. Join a breed society, club or organization and become an active member. If you are a good public speaker, put together an interesting talk about your farm and livestock. Support this with pics or a video.

Some producers hold seminars or run courses on farm. This allows them to promote their industry and, at the same time, display and market their own stock. Others offer their professional expertise as tutors at colleges and evening classes.

If you prefer writing to speaking, send an article to your local paper or livestock magazine. Editors are always looking for fresh and interesting pieces about local people and events.

3. *Advertise yourself*

Letter-headed paper is easy to print at home. Business cards can be produced very cheaply these days. They are a prerequisite for any small business.

Have an annual budget for promotional expenses. Stay within your budget. If you can afford novelty promotional items such as calendars, postcards or fridge magnets, always make them attractive so people will keep them. Have your logo and stud name embroidered on your T-shirts and caps.

Have glossy advertising leaflets printed and ready to hand out at events or, if that is too expensive, print the information on an A4 sheet on your home computer. Provide details of your stock with prices if possible (some people are embarrassed to ask). Also make up a sheet of basic husbandry information to hand to new breeders. Provide a book list of recommended reading material.

Besides your primary produce, always promote any bi-products from your animals such as fur, feathers, oils, hair, milk or meat, even goat knick-knacks that you sell on the farm. Advertise these items at shows.

4. *Breed societies*

Most livestock types are represented by breed societies. By becoming a member you will have access to up-to-date information and meet more people. By being an active member you will gain respect from fellow breeders, but do not expect the society to market your animals for you.

Some people enter new and alternate livestock enterprises believing that once they have the animals *it will all happen*. Then, when they find that they cannot sell their stock they ask, "What is the society doing for me?"

These are the types of people who do not last long in any business. They sell up and leave giving that industry a bad name.

Only through positive participation and enthusiasm will any single venture or group grow.

5. *Promotion at shows*

Agricultural shows and local events are an inexpensive way of promoting yourself and your animals to the public. If your breed society is participating at a show then get involved and take your livestock along. Enter competitions or offer to sponsor a prize. Winning an award or prize is effective promotion.

When you show you animals ensure they well groomed and that you present yourself in a smart and professional manner. You are on show too. Likewise, the animal pens and holding areas should be neat and tidy. Display a professionally made sign bearing your logo.

At agricultural shows, prospective breeders want information.

Provide an eye-catching display board of photographs (preferably enlargements) and a table for your business cards and hand-outs. Be available to talk to people and always observe professional courtesy.

Don't forget to record the names and addresses of anyone interested in entering the business and, more importantly, follow these up with a phone call or email when you have more stock available for sale.

If you have not reached the stage of entering animals in the larger shows, try the local events. These often welcome displays of animals free of charge but you may have to provide your own small stock pen. These are not difficult to construct from a few sheets of mesh.

The biggest attraction at these events is often young animals – they promote themselves but, remember, promotion starts with you.

6. *Advertising signs*

Signs on vehicles provide excellent publicity. If you are transporting stock why not promote your stud name on your vehicle or trailer. If your do not want a permanent sign on the car door then consider a custom made spare-tyre cover or portable sign for the trailer.

Have a sign made for your vehicle. You have, no doubt, heard of the *Batmobile* – I called mine *The Goatmobile*.

Roadside and farm signs bring visitors onto the farm. The costs are not high and this type of promotion is worthwhile.

7. *Other advertisements*

When you have stock for sale, advertise it in the press. Small lineage ads placed regularly in appropriate papers will have better results than a single full-page spread with no follow up. Some papers offer free adverts.

Advertise on the internet. Regular advertising pays dividends.

8. *Makes ever post a winner*

If you are planning an interstate or overseas holiday consider finding out, before you leave, if there are any breeders located near your holiday destination. Try contacting the secretary of the breed society for the state or country that you will be visiting for a list of breeders.

People involved in the same venture as you are usually delighted to meet you. Always write or ring first. You can pick up new ideas from seeing how other people conduct their farms. Physical, as well as electronic networking keeps you up to date with what is going on in the industry.

If a breeder is planning an Artificial Insemination program or shearing or vaccination day, why not volunteer to help. You will learn a lot from hands on experience or from just observing.

9. *Promote through sponsorship*

It's not always easy to get sponsorship but it costs nothing to try. Local rural traders and feed merchants may be happy to sponsor you in a modest way.

While these are a few promotional ideas, there are many more worth remembering:
1. Success in any rural business does not happen overnight and stock will not sell themselves.
2. Be professional in the way you market your product. Define your objectives and work out a promotional plan.
3. Make use of any market research data available.
4. Always stay positive and remember that promotion is an investment in your future.

Note: While this article is directed at goat breeders, the same marketing/promotional tactics apply to sheep or alpaca studs, aqua-culturists, vermiculturalists, plant nurserymen and more.

Conclusion

The Spirit of the Goat

With thanks to Robert Dunn for this image (New Zealand)

As breeders, one thing we all share is a genuine regard for goats and we cannot help but admire their indomitable spirit of freedom. This characteristic is epitomised in this old French poem.

Prayer of the Goat

Lord,
Let me live as I will
I need a little wild freedom
A little gladness of heart
The Strange Taste of unknown flowers
For whom else are your mountains?
Your snow, wind? – The springs?
The sheep do not understand
They graze and graze

All of them
And always in the same direction
And then eternally
Chew the cud of Your marvels,
Leap Your chasms
And, mouth stuffed
With intoxicating grasses
Quiver with an adventurers delight
On the summit of the world.

Amen

From the book, Prayers from the Ark (1947), written by Carmen Bernos de Gasztold and translated from the French by Rumer Godden.

I hope you found something of interest in this little book no matter what stage you are at in the goat industry.

Though some of the photographs were taken by the author, I thank the other sources from which I have acquired images, in particular the Tambookie Boer Goat Stud in Western Australia.

GOATS contains material written by the author over several years and first published in *The Goat Farmer* magazine. Where possible, the original information has been updated.